4/2

ENDANGERED
KOMODO DRAGONS

Bobbie Kalman

Crabtree Publishing Company

www.crabtreebooks.com

Earth's Endangered Animals Series
A Bobbie Kalman Book

Dedicated by Reagan Miller
For my mom and dad, with my love and appreciation, always

Editor-in-Chief
Bobbie Kalman

Writing team
Bobbie Kalman
Reagan Miller

Substantive editors
Amanda Bishop
Kelley MacAulay

Editors
Molly Aloian
Kristina Lundblad
Kathryn Smithyman

Art director
Robert MacGregor

Design
Katherine Kantor

Production coordinator
Katherine Kantor

Photo research
Crystal Foxton

Consultant
Patricia Loesche, Ph.D., Animal Behavior Program,
Department of Psychology, University of Washington

Photographs
ardea.com: Adrian Warren: pages 19, 22;
   Masahiro Iijima: page 24
Bruce Coleman Inc.: Norman Tomalin: pages 4, 13;
   Erwin & Peggy Bauer: page 5;
   Valerie Taylor: page 16
Boyd Norton/Evergreen Photo Alliance: page 20
Joe McDonald: page 9
Minden Pictures: Tui De Roy: pages 6, 15, 25;
   Mark Jones: pages 7, 11;
   Mitsuaki Iwago: page 17
© Michael Pitts/naturepl.com: title page, pages 14, 23, 28
Tom Stack & Associates: Manfred Gottschalk: page 29
©Wolfgang Kaehler, www.wkaehlerphoto.com: pages 18, 27
Other images by Corel and Digital Stock

Illustrations
Barbara Bedell: back cover, pages 7, 10-11, 12, 14, 31
Katherine Kantor: border, pages 5, 15

Crabtree Publishing Company

www.crabtreebooks.com   1-800-387-7650

Copyright © **2005 CRABTREE PUBLISHING COMPANY.**
All rights reserved. No part of this publication may be
reproduced, stored in a retrieval system or be transmitted in
any form or by any means, electronic, mechanical, photocopying,
recording, or otherwise, without the prior written permission
of Crabtree Publishing Company. In Canada: We acknowledge the
financial support of the Government of Canada through the Book
Publishing Industry Development Program (BPIDP) for our
publishing activities.

Cataloging-in-Publication Data
Kalman, Bobbie.
  Endangered Komodo dragons / Bobbie Kalman.
    p. cm. -- (Earth's endangered animals series)
  Includes index.
  ISBN 0-7787-1857-3 (RLB) -- ISBN 0-7787-1903-0 (pbk.)
  1. Komodo dragon--Juvenile literature. 2. Endangered species--
Juvenile literature. I. Title.
  QL666.L29K25 2004
  597.95'968--dc22

2004011115
LC

**Published in
the United States**
PMB 16A
350 Fifth Ave.
Suite 3308
New York, NY
10118

**Published
in Canada**
616 Welland Ave.
St. Catharines, Ontario
Canada
L2M 5V6

**Published in the
United Kingdom**
White Cross Mills
High Town
Lancaster, LA1 4XS
United Kingdom

**Published
in Australia**
386 Mt. Alexander Rd.
Ascot Vale (Melbourne)
VIC 3032

Contents

Endangered animals

Today, there are more than 1,000 known **species**, or types, of animals that are **endangered**. Endangered animals are at risk of disappearing from the Earth forever. If endangered animals are not protected, they may become **extinct**. Extinct animals no longer live on Earth.

Animals at risk

There is only one species of Komodo dragon, and it is **vulnerable**. There are only a few thousand of these animals still alive. Komodo dragons are in trouble because they live in a very small area of the world. Keep reading to find out more about why Komodo dragons are in trouble.

Scientists believe there are 3,000 to 5,000 Komodo dragons left in the world. If people do not work to protect Komodo dragons, they may soon become endangered.

Named after a myth

Komodo dragons look like the fierce, fire-breathing dragons people have written about in fairy tales. Fairy-tale dragons often had special powers, and most were fierce. Perhaps some of these stories were inspired by Komodo dragons, which are also fierce.

4

Words to know

Scientists use special words to describe animals in danger. Some of these words are listed below.

vulnerable Describes animals that may soon become endangered

endangered Describes animals that are in danger of dying out in the **wild**, or the natural places where they live

critically endangered Describes animals that are at a high risk of dying out in the wild

extinct Describes animals that have died out everywhere or have not been seen alive for at least 50 years

What are Komodo dragons?

The largest Komodo dragons can grow to be more than ten feet (3 m) long.

Komodo dragons belong to a group of animals called **reptiles**. Alligators and crocodiles are other reptiles. Reptiles are **cold-blooded**. The body temperatures of cold-blooded animals change as the temperatures of their surroundings change.

Monitor lizards

Komodo dragons are **lizards**. Lizards are reptiles that have two pairs of legs, long bodies, and tails. Komodo dragons are the largest lizards in the world! They belong to a group of lizards called **monitors**. There are over 40 species of monitor lizards. All monitors have heavy bodies, long tails, sharp claws, and strong legs.

Ancient relatives

The Komodo dragon is a distant relative of the **mosasaur**. Mosasaurs were **prehistoric** reptiles that lived in oceans. They were fierce hunters that fed on birds, fish, and squid. They were very large. Some were over 30 feet (9 m) long. Mosasaurs became extinct over 65 million years ago. The **Megalania** is another ancient relative of the Komodo dragon. It was a giant monitor lizard that lived on land 25,000 years ago. It looked a lot like a Komodo dragon but may have been larger. The name Megalania means "ancient giant butcher." Scientists believe this animal ate **mammals**, birds, and other reptiles.

mosasaur

A Komodo dragon's habitat

A **habitat** is the natural place where an animal lives. Komodo dragon habitats include both land and water. Komodo dragons live in Indonesia, mainly on four small islands called Flores, Rintja, Gili Motang, and Komodo. The islands are surrounded by the Indian Ocean.

The islands are covered with rocky mountains and grassy areas called **tropical savannas**. They are very hot and dry, and they often have **droughts**. Droughts are long periods of time without rain. Very few animals live on these islands because of the heat and droughts.

Komodo dragons are named after Komodo Island, one of the islands on which they live.

In the ocean

Komodo dragons are strong swimmers. They often swim from one island to another. The beaches of the islands are an important part of dragon habitats. The dragons search the beaches for **marine birds** and dead fish to eat.

Komodo dragon bodies

Adult Komodo dragons have powerful bodies. Most grow to a length of nine feet (2.7 m). Their bodies are covered with tough, thick skin. The skin is gray and brown.

Deadly mouths

Komodo dragons are famous for their deadly mouths! Tiny living things called **bacteria** live in them. The bacteria are deadly to almost every animal that comes in contact with them—every animal, that is, except the Komodo dragon! Scientists are studying the bodies of Komodo dragons to learn why the bacteria do not harm them.

The lower jaws of Komodo dragons open very wide. The wide mouths allow komodo dragons to swallow huge chunks of unchewed food.

Komodo dragons have about 60 razor-sharp teeth hidden under their gums. Old or damaged teeth often fall out, but new teeth soon grow in to replace them.

Tasting scent

When a Komodo dragon hunts, it tastes the air with its tongue. It flicks its **forked** tongue in and out of its mouth to gather scents from the air. The dragon then pushes its tongue against its **Jacobson's organ**, which is a sensitive patch on the roof of its mouth. By touching its tongue to the Jacobson's organ, the Komodo dragon can taste the scent. This scent tells the dragon if food is nearby.

*Komodo dragons use their sharp claws to climb trees, grasp **prey**, and dig **burrows**, or small caves.*

The tail of a Komodo dragon is about as long as the length of the rest of its body. Dragons use their tails to move themselves forward as they swim. They also swing their strong tails at other dragons during fights.

11

A Komodo dragon's life cycle

Every animal goes through a set of changes called a **life cycle**. A life cycle is made up of all the changes that happen to an animal from the time it is born to the time it becomes an adult that can make babies of its own. With each baby, a new life cycle begins.

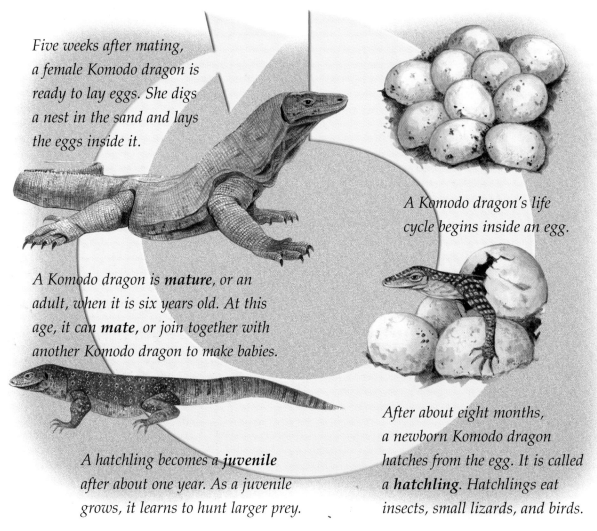

Five weeks after mating, a female Komodo dragon is ready to lay eggs. She digs a nest in the sand and lays the eggs inside it.

A Komodo dragon's life cycle begins inside an egg.

*A Komodo dragon is **mature**, or an adult, when it is six years old. At this age, it can **mate**, or join together with another Komodo dragon to make babies.*

*A hatchling becomes a **juvenile** after about one year. As a juvenile grows, it learns to hunt larger prey.*

*After about eight months, a newborn Komodo dragon hatches from the egg. It is called a **hatchling**. Hatchlings eat insects, small lizards, and birds.*

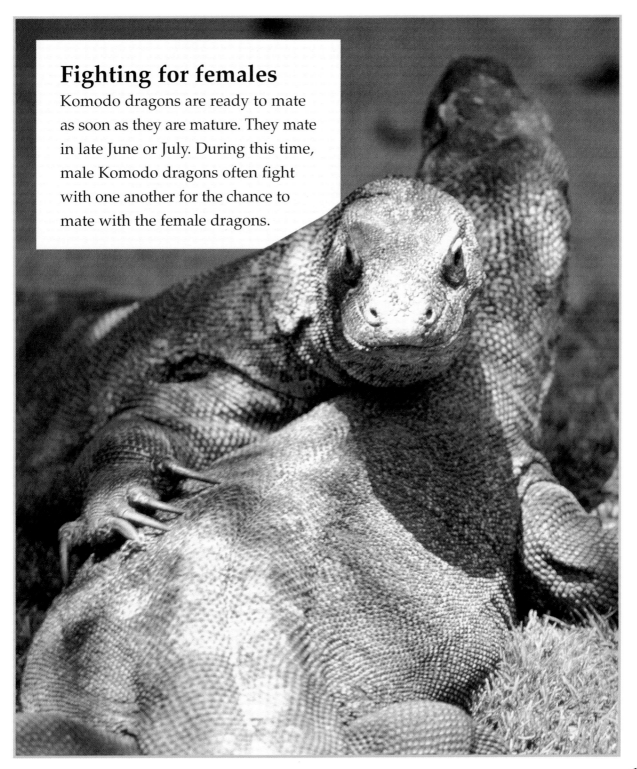

Fighting for females

Komodo dragons are ready to mate as soon as they are mature. They mate in late June or July. During this time, male Komodo dragons often fight with one another for the chance to mate with the female dragons.

Staying alive!

Predators are animals that hunt and eat other animals. Wild dogs and adult Komodo dragons eat Komodo dragon hatchlings. The hatchlings use their habitats to keep them safe from predators. As soon as they hatch from their eggs, the young dragons climb up into nearby trees.

The hatchlings are brightly colored, so they blend in with the colors of the trees. Predators cannot see them, and adult dragons cannot climb the trees to reach them. Hatchlings live in trees because they cannot protect themselves yet.

14

A cool home

When they are large enough to protect themselves from predators on the ground, Komodo dragons leave the trees and move into burrows underground. Staying underground keeps Komodo dragons cool.

Komodo dragons dig their own burrows or use burrows made by other animals, such as porcupines or boars. Some Komodo dragons have many burrows, whereas others have only one.

Food fit for a dragon

Komodo dragons hunt and eat mainly Rusa deer. They also hunt birds, wild pigs, monkeys, and other reptiles. The dragons eat nearly all parts of their prey, including the bones, hooves, and fur.

After a large meal, a Komodo dragon does not need to eat again for several days. It also does not need to drink water for many days after eating. It gets most of the water it needs from the prey it has eaten.

*A Komodo dragon's stomach **expands**, or stretches, to make room for a large meal. A Komodo dragon can eat an entire deer in one meal!*

Lying in wait

A Komodo dragon is a smart and patient hunter. It often hides for hours in tall grasses near a water hole. It waits for prey that come to drink at the hole. When an animal walks toward the water, the Komodo dragon uses its powerful legs to pounce on the prey. It then knocks the animal to the ground and bites it with its sharp teeth.

A brief escape

When the Komodo dragon bites its prey, the animal's wound fills with deadly bacteria from the Komodo dragon's mouth. If the animal gets away from the dragon after being bitten, it soon dies from the bacteria. The Komodo dragon uses its Jacobson's organ to track down the dying animal. It then feeds on the dead body.

Komodo dragons also find food by tracking the scents of wounded animals.

Komodo dragons in groups

Komodo dragons spend most of their time alone. If a Komodo dragon hunts and kills an animal, it does not share its meal with another Komodo dragon. Komodo dragons sometimes gather together to eat **carrion**, however. Carrion is the meat of animals that are already dead.

During these feedings, the largest and strongest dragons eat first. Young Komodo dragons stay away from the feeding area until the older animals have finished eating. A young dragon that dares to go near a hungry adult may be attacked or even be eaten!

Sending messages

When they are in groups, Komodo dragons **communicate** with one another by making sounds. They often show anger by hissing loudly. This hissing sound warns other dragons to stay away.

Komodo dragons also show anger by moving their bodies in certain ways. For example, they sometimes puff up the loose skin around their necks to make themselves look bigger. Komodo dragons also whip their tails from side to side to scare off other dragons.

More people, less space

Scientists discovered Komodo dragons in 1912. Even then, they worried that these animals might not be able to stay alive in such a small area of the world. Since 1912, the number of people who share the four islands with the Komodo dragons has grown. People take up a lot of space. As a result, there is less space for the Komodo dragons and other animals to live. The space in which Komodo dragons must now live is too small for these large reptiles.

*Villagers on the islands of Komodo and Flores must take special care to avoid meeting Komodo dragons. Their homes are built on high **stilts**, or poles, to keep out the dragons.*

Losing land

People on the islands need places to live and food to eat. They **clear** land in order to build homes. They also grow food such as wheat and rice on some of the land. As people continue to take over more of the land, the Komodo dragons lose more of their habitats.

21

Problems finding enough food

People clear land by setting fire to the grass and plants. When they burn these plants, they are burning the food of animals such as deer and wild pigs. Many of these animals die of **starvation**, or lack of food. After a while, there are not enough of these animals for Komodo dragons to eat. People also hunt deer and wild pigs for food. When there are fewer deer and wild pigs, Komodo dragons have less food, and many of them starve.

This Komodo dragon is very thin because it cannot find enough food to eat. If it does not find food soon, it may die of starvation.

Into the villages

When their usual prey becomes hard to find, Komodo dragons hunt other animals to survive. The Komodo dragons often enter villages and kill **livestock**, or animals that people raise for food, such as goats. To prevent their livestock from being eaten, some villagers shoot and kill Komodo dragons. Many people also kill Komodo dragons by leaving out poisoned meat for them to eat.

Food for feral dogs

Hunters often bring **feral**, or wild, dogs with them to the islands to help them track deer. The hunters leave many of the dogs on the islands. Like Komodo dragons, feral dogs feed on deer. With people and dogs feeding on the deer, there will soon be too few deer for Komodo dragons to eat.

Many local fishers lay their fish out on the beach to dry them in the sun. Komodo dragons often catch the scent of the fish and go to the beach to feed on them.

23

People and poaching

Poachers are people who **illegally** hunt and kill animals, including Komodo dragons. They sell the body parts of Komodo dragons for money. The body parts are used to make special medicines. Some people believe that these medicines will help them become better swimmers or stop them from growing older. There is no proof that the medicines work! Today, it is against the law to sell the body parts of Komodo dragons, but some people continue to break this law.

Kidnapped Komodos

In recent years, **animal traders** have started trapping many Komodo dragons. Animal traders are people who capture animals illegally and sell them as pets. People pay animal traders thousands of dollars for young Komodo dragons, but Komodo dragons are very difficult to raise as pets. Most of the dragons that are taken from their natural homes die soon after they are captured.

Juvenile Komodo dragons are often captured by animal traders.

Protecting Komodo dragons

Many people want to help Komodo dragons. The government of Indonesia created Komodo National Park in 1980 to help save these reptiles. The park includes the islands of Komodo, Rintja, and Padar, as well as several other small islands. The protected land provides safe homes for Komodo dragons and many other animals, such as Timor deer and orange-footed scrub owls. Komodo National Park also protects the plants and animals that live on the **coasts** of the islands. A coast is an area where an ocean meets land.

More than 18,000 tourists visit Komodo National Park each year.

Defending the dragons

Komodo National Park **rangers** guard Komodo dragons in the park from poachers and animal traders. They also control the number of deer hunted by villagers to make sure that the Komodo dragons have enough food to eat. The rangers take people on tours of the park and educate them about Komodo dragons. Park rangers and scientists work together to study Komodo dragons in their natural habitats. By learning more about Komodo dragons, they can find new ways to protect these amazing animals.

Scientists and zookeepers from all over the world are working to increase the **population**, or number, of Komodo dragons. In 1992, a healthy group of Komodo dragons hatched at the National Zoo in Washington, D.C. It was the first time hatchlings born outside Indonesia survived.

Since then, about 95 Komodo dragons have hatched in zoos across North America. These births are important in helping to keep the species alive. Scientists at zoos know how to keep Komodo dragons safe and healthy. They also study these animals to learn more about them.

Safe zoo habitats

Although many zoos are helping Komodo dragons, some do not provide proper habitats for these unusual animals. Komodo dragons that live in these zoos often become sick, and some even die. To protect Komodo dragons, the Indonesian government limits the number of dragons that can be captured and taken to zoos outside Indonesia. Only zoos that give animals the best care are allowed to keep Komodo dragons. The president of Indonesia is the only person who can give zoos permission to raise Komodo dragons.

The Komodo dragon is Indonesia's national animal.

Dragons on display

Komodo dragons are fascinating animals! There is a lot more to learn about them. For example, did you know that Komodo dragons can run up to fifteen miles per hour (24.1 kph), or that they can eat over five pounds (2.3 kg) of food per minute? You and your classmates can share what you have learned with other students at your school by writing stories and poems about Komodo dragons. You can even create a bulletin board in your school that compares Komodo dragons with fairy-tale dragons!

Healthy Komodo dragons can live up to 30 years in the wild, as long as they are not put in danger.

Surfing for Komodos

There are many fun ways to learn more about these incredible lizards. Visit your local library to find books, videos, and magazines about Komodo dragons. You can also search the Internet. Below are two great Komodo dragon websites:

- www.thebigzoo.com/Animals/Komodo_Dragon.asp
- www.sandiegozoo.org/animalbytes/t-komodo.html

Glossary

Note: Boldfaced words that are defined in the text may not appear in the glossary.

bacteria Tiny living things that can cause diseases

clear To remove trees, shrubs, and other plant life from an area

communicate To send messages by using sounds and signs

forked Split into two parts

illegally Describing an act that is carried out against the law

mammal A warm-blooded animal that gives birth to live young

marine bird A bird that lives near the ocean

prehistoric Describing animals that existed before the beginning of recorded history

prey An animal that is hunted and eaten by other animals

reptile A cold-blooded animal that lays eggs

tropical savanna An area in a hot, dry climate that is covered mainly with grass and shrubs

wild Natural places where plants and animals live, which are not controlled by people

Index

2 3 4 5 6 7 8 9 0 Printed in the U.S.A. 4 3 2 1 0 9 8 7 6